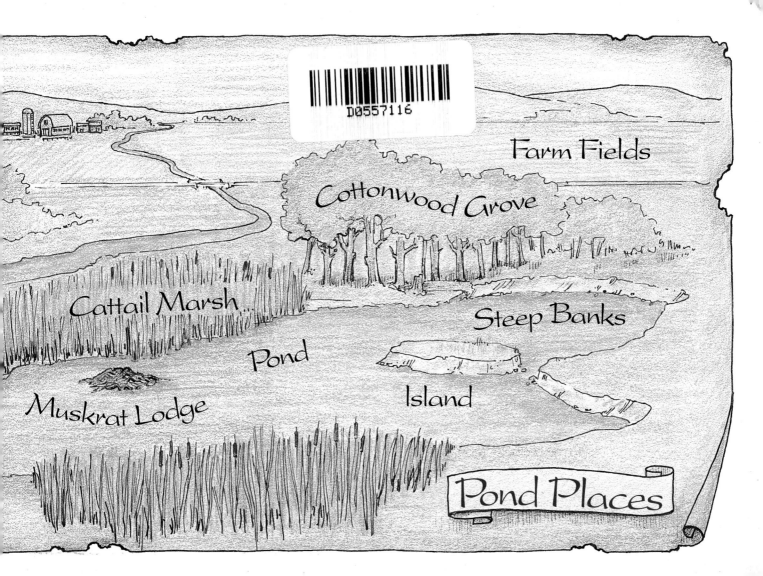

Farm Fields

Cottonwood Grove

Cattail Marsh

Steep Banks

Pond

Island

Muskrat Lodge

Pond Places

To Michael. Remember snorkeling after turtles in Burntside Lake?—Mom-Ann

The animals and plants illustrated in this book occur widely in ponds and marshes across North America. Your pond may not have *all* these species, but it will probably have most of them or their look-alikes. The selected species have been reviewed and approved by scientists at the Denver Museum of Natural History.

We wish to thank Dr. Charles Preston, Curator of Ornithology at the Denver Museum of Natural History, who checked this book for scientific accuracy. We also wish to thank Dr. Michael J. Weissmann, Faculty Affiliate, Department of Bioagricultural Sciences and Pest Management, Colorado State University, who reviewed the facts on insects.

Book design by Jill Soukup

Library of Congress Cataloging-in-Publication Data
Cooper, Ann (Ann C.)
    Around the pond / Ann Cooper ; illustrated by Dorothy Emerling.
       p.   cm. -- (Wild wonders series)
      Summary: Examines the interdependent lives of the various animals and plants that inhabit various parts of a pond from the surface film of the water to its weedy depths.
    ISBN 1-57098-223-6 (pbk.)
    1. Pond animals--Juvenile literature. [1. Pond animals. 2. Pond plants.
3. Pond ecology. 4. Ecology.]   I. Emerling, Dorothy, ill. II. Title. III. Series.
QL146.3.C66 1998
591.763'6--dc21
                                        98-25065
                                           CIP
                                           AC

Published by the Denver Museum of Natural History Press
2001 Colorado Boulevard, Denver, Colorado 80205 www.dmnh.org
in cooperation with Roberts Rinehart Publishers
6309 Monarch Park Place, Niwot, Colorado 80503
Tel. 303.652.2685 Fax 303.652.2689 www.robertsrinehart.com

Distributed in Ireland and the U.K. by Roberts Rinehart Publishers
Trinity House, Charleston Road, Dublin 6, Ireland
Distributed to the trade by Publishers Group West

Printed in Hong Kong

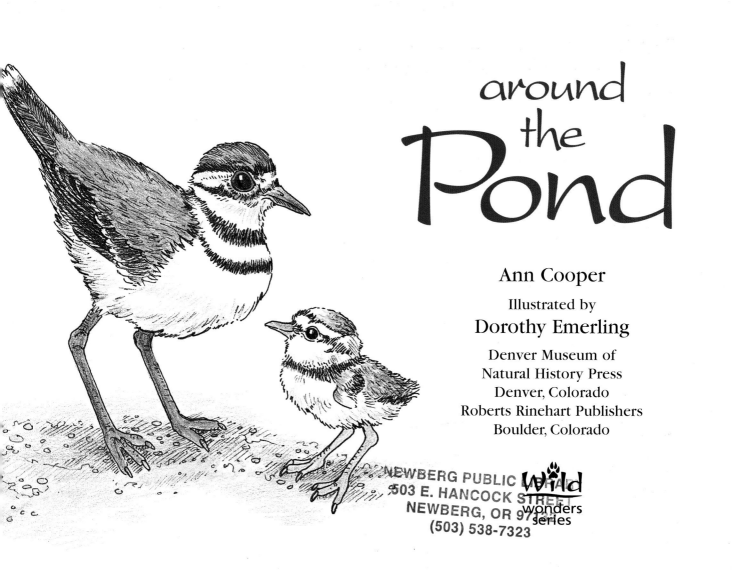

around the Pond

Ann Cooper

Illustrated by
Dorothy Emerling

Denver Museum of
Natural History Press
Denver, Colorado
Roberts Rinehart Publishers
Boulder, Colorado

Wild
wonders
series

Spring Fever

Swirls of snow drift over farm fields and meadows.
The pond lies locked in ice. The only sign of life is
a lacy, paw-print trail from the woods to the marsh—
until one sunny day, spring blows in on a warm wind.
It wakes the pond, bringing begin-again fever.

Ducks become jittery. They chase across the pond, all skitter,
splash, and quack. Long V's of geese fly in from the south,
honking. They use their webbed feet as brakes. Splashdown!
Small birds flit everywhere. The marsh is loud with
twittering. The air is musky-damp. It smells of growing.

What makes the pond such a noisy, busy place?

A pond is full of hideaways: tangled waterweed jungles, dense cattails, muddy-buggy shorelines, fallen logs, lily pads, nest-safe islands, steep banks for dens, and shady trees. In water and on land, there are scores of places to live and raise a family.

Marshy edges and wet meadows nearby soak up rain and melting snow like a giant sponge. The moisture helps plants sprout. Water drains into the pond, carrying with it soil, minerals, and dead plants and animals. They act like pond vitamins, making nutritious pond "soup." On land and in water, pond habitats grow lots of food: roots and shoots, seeds and weeds, prey for predators, and especially insects galore.

No wonder so many creatures choose to live here!

Froggy Went A-Courting

Bullfrog spent the winter at the bottom of the pond, not moving, not eating. His body was as cold as the mud in which he hid. As the spring sun warmed the pond, Bullfrog stirred from his muddy hideout. He kicked his chilly legs and swam slowly up, up.

For hours he sprawled in a tangle of pondweed near the surface, basking. He kept watch, his bulgy golden eyes just above the water, alert for danger. Until he was toasty, he could not swim fast, or leap far, or escape from hungry herons or raccoons.

Time passed. Bullfrog felt strong and fast, ready to go courting. One night he swam to his finest weed patch. *Bur-rum, bur-rum,* he croaked in his deep voice. All around him frog-songs rumbled and clicked in the steamy evening air. He called again, *Bur-rum,* trying to make his voice heard in the din.

At last! A female swam over and touched him, excited by his fine voice. He grabbed her from behind in a hug. She laid her jelly-eggs. As the eggs streamed out, Bullfrog fertilized them with his sperm so they would grow. He let go of this mate. *Bur-rum, bur-rum.* With his mighty voice, he would charm many mates tonight!

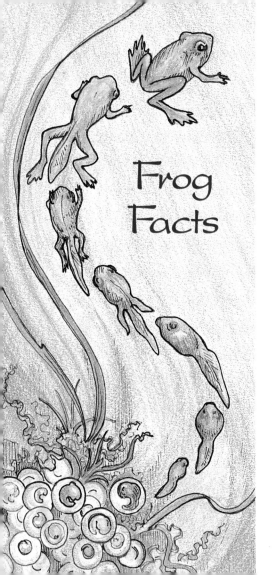

Frog Facts

Jelly-Eggs

Bullfrog females lay clusters of up to 20,000 eggs. In a week or so, the eggs hatch into wiggly-tailed tadpoles.

Tadpole Tales

Bullfrog tadpoles eat algae (green slime). As they grow, their tails shrink, their legs sprout, and they become tiny frogs. The change takes two years.

Breathing

Tadpoles breathe with gills, like fish. Frogs use their lungs, like people. Frogs also breathe through their moist skin.

On the Menu

Most frogs eat insects, spiders, worms, and other small prey. They catch insects with a quick zap of their long tongues.

Ears, Eyes, Nose

A frog's ears are flat circles, like drum skins, near its eyes. A frog's eyes and nostrils are high on its head. It can see and breathe when it is mostly underwater and hard for predators to see from above.

Noise by Boys

Only male frogs call to attract mates. Chorus frogs make sounds like a fingernail scraping the teeth of a comb. Leopard frogs "snore." All scared frogs squawk or croak when they jump back into the pond.

Snack Attack

Bullfrogs, the largest frogs in North America, eat mice, baby birds, lizards, snakes, fish, snails, and small frogs!

Toad or Frog?

Toads and frogs are amphibians. They can live both on land and in water. Toads have warty skin. Frogs have slimy skin. Slimy skin stops a frog from drying out on land and makes the frog slippery for enemies to catch. Some frog slime has a bad taste. Some is even poisonous.

Enemies

Herons, rats, snakes, raccoons, fish, turtles, mink, larger frogs, and some people eat adult frogs. Dragonfly larvae, water beetles, fish, newts, and birds eat tadpoles. Leeches and insects eat frog eggs.

The Best Nest

Blackbird was so-o busy collecting leaves and grass to weave her nest. She had chosen a site in the marsh where the water was deep enough to keep her nest safe. She strung her nest between dead cattail stalks, weaving each strand tightly around the stems so the nest would not slip or tip. It was a strong, deep cup. She lined it with mud and bits of fine grass. After five days, her nest was ready.

She laid four blue eggs. For eleven days she kept them snug under her warm body. She left them only while she pecked a quick snack. At last, her chicks hatched. What scrawny, wobbly scraps they were—all beaks and squawk!

While Blackbird built her nest and incubated her eggs, her mate sat high on a cattail, squawking. *Kon-karee, kon-karee,* he called, lifting his wings and flashing his bright shoulder feathers. He was boss of this cattail patch, and his job was to make sure all the other blackbirds knew it! If other males flew into his space, he called, flashed, and chased them away. But when big birds—crows and hawks—flew by, he ganged up with the other male blackbirds to send the big birds off. That way, they could all keep their families safe.

About Blackbirds

Working Mom

A female blackbird's job doesn't end when her eggs hatch. She brings food for her chicks until they leave the nest. She carries their fecal sacs (poop) and drops them far from the nest to keep it clean.

Oops!

Sometimes a hammock-nest tips when the stems that support it grow unevenly. Eggs topple out. Some chicks die when they fall out of the nest before they can fly. Snapping turtles or fish eat them.

Neighbors

Wrens, song sparrows, and warblers also nest around the marsh.

Looks

Male red-winged blackbirds are flashy so they can attract mates and show other males the space is taken. Females are drab and streaky so they won't give away their nest sites.

Blackbird Rivals

In ponds and marshes in the West, yellow-headed blackbirds push the redwings out, taking the best waterfront nest sites.

Enemies

Hawks, owls, and crows prey on blackbirds or their chicks. Foxes, mink, raccoons, and weasels take eggs and nestlings— if they can get to them. Water snakes slither up to nests, too.

Food

Blackbirds eat all kinds of insects. Caterpillars and mayflies are favorites. They also eat all kinds of seeds.

Winter

Blackbirds leave the pond in winter. They glean (gather) grain and weed seeds in fields and roost in noisy treetop flocks.

Skunked

Dusk was falling, bats flitting, as Mother Skunk left her leaf-lined den below a fallen tree in the cottonwood grove. Her five playful youngsters followed in a line, staying close. This was their first outing. Outside was a scary place.

Snuffle, sniffle, snuffle. As she waddled along, Mother Skunk poked her pointy nose into the soil to sniff out beetles, worms, and other tasty food. The little ones copied her, poking and scrabbling. Their tiny noses twitched and quivered with excitement.

The smallest one, last in line, pounced on a beetle. The other youngsters scuttled back to have a look. *Crunch!* Smallest One ate the beetle before his litter mates could wrestle it away.

Mother Skunk ambled down a worn trail to the pond. She knew a good place to hunt for turtle eggs. As she came to the bank, she stopped short. A fox! Next-in-line Baby almost crashed into her.

Mother Skunk strutted toward Fox, her legs stiff. She lifted her tail high, showing off her elegant white stripes. She stamped her feet once, twice. Fox backed away from his duck-feast, his muzzle feathery. He knew that high-rise tail! He knew there was no enemy fiercer or smellier than a protective mother skunk. Phew! He had met that awful stink before.

Skunk Snippets

Warning!

Black and white are tip-off colors that remind enemies to leave skunks alone. If they don't, the skunk squirts its stinky spray as far as twelve feet, accurately! Spray stings the enemy's eyes and makes it feel sick and gag. The smell lasts for days.

The foul, oily liquid squirts from two marble-size glands near the skunk's tail.

Skunks try their spray against cars, too. Of course, it does not work! Many skunks become roadkill.

Family Life

Skunks raise their five to nine babies in ground dens lined with grasses. The babies are mouse-size at birth. They can spray by two weeks old, even before their eyes open, even before they grow sharp teeth and thick, glossy fur.

Chow Time!

Skunks are omnivorous. They eat almost anything: grasshoppers, beetles, voles, mice, turtle eggs, fruit, grain, berries, and vegetables.

Skunks also eat the eggs of birds, such as ducks and coot, that nest on the ground. They crack open large eggs by throwing them back through their legs to hit a hard surface.

Enemies

Skunks have such a good defense that few enemies seek them out. Eagles, coyotes, foxes, bobcats, and badgers sometimes eat them. Great horned owls hunt them more often. (Owls have a poor sense of smell.)

Travelers

Skunks may travel far on the hunt. They bed down for a day's sleep wherever they happen to be—in brush piles, culverts, abandoned fox or coyote dens, hollow logs, even under people's porches.

Tree Nests

Wood ducks nest in tree cavities. Their eggs are safe from skunks. When the chicks are ready to leave the nest, they take a giant leap!

Little Monster

Dragonfly Nymph skulked in the waterweeds. He watched the mosquito wigglers hanging from the surface of the pond. Before, he would have feasted on them. Today he was not hungry. He did not even move when a plump tadpole wiggled by. His outside skeleton felt tight. It was time to shed one last skin, time to take to the air.

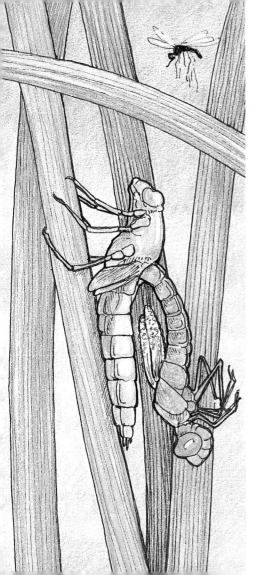

Claw by claw, he pulled himself up a bulrush stem. He kept climbing until he was well clear of the water and any hungry, jumping fish. Clinging with his six feet, he tensed his body muscles. His too-tight skin split along the back. Slowly, he struggled out of his old shell. At first his wings were milky-pale and crumpled. He pumped "blood" into his wing veins until the wings stiffened and spread.

For two hours he dangled from the remains of his old skin, waiting for his wings to harden. Zoom! He hurtled into the buggy air to hunt. He ate mosquitoes and midges in the air. But when he caught a moth, he zipped back to perch on a cattail. He clipped off the moth's wings and ate its soft body.

Dragonfly Details

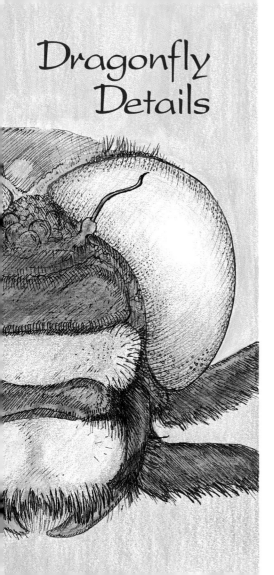

What Big Eyes . . .

A dragonfly's eyes are so big they take up its whole head. The eyes are compound eyes. Each has thousands of seeing cells, or facets, which see a tiny part of the view. Together they see a complete picture.

Exoskeleton

Outside skeletons do not stretch. A nymph sheds its hard skin every time it needs growing room. It may live in the water for 2 or more years and shed up to 15 times.

Jet-propelled

Dragonfly nymphs take in water through their tails and breathe oxygen from it. They can also squirt the water out in a jet to scoot themselves away from predators.

Dragon or Damsel?

A dragonfly perches with its wings out to the side. A damselfly folds its wings over its body.

Fossil Record

Long before dinosaurs lived, huge dragonflies with two-foot wingspans flew in the swamps.

Mating Time

A male dragonfly grabs the back of his female's head with his claspers. She curls her tail under his body to get sperm to make her eggs grow. The two often fly joined until the female lays her eggs in a plant stem, in wet wood, or in the pond.

Flight Champions!

Dragonflies fly much faster than you could peddle your bicycle! They zip to and fro or hover like helicopters, moving their four wings independently.

Eat . . .

A dragonfly is a fierce predator at all stages of its life. A nymph (larva) eats insects, tadpoles, and even small fish. It grabs prey by shooting out its spoonlike, bristle-tipped lower jaw. An adult dragonfly catches its insect prey in the air by forming its bristly legs into a basket.

. . . Or Be Eaten

A dragonfly is also prey at all stages of its life. Water birds, snakes, frogs, turtles, fish, and big insects eat nymphs. Birds, frogs, and turtles catch dragonfly adults, especially newly hatched ones that cannot fly well yet.

Grab a Ride!

Mother Grebe was on nest duty when her chicks hatched. One by one, they pecked out of their eggshells. At first their downy feathers were spiky and damp. In the warm air, they soon dried. The chicks looked like little striped fuzz balls. Soon, they wanted food.

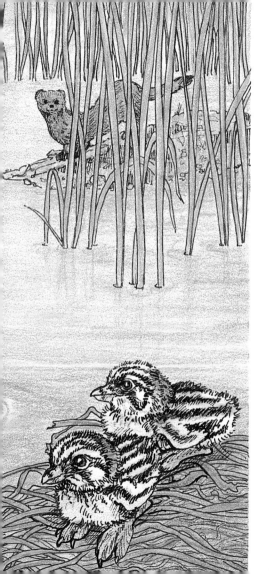

Mother Grebe clucked softly for her chicks to follow and slipped off her nest into the water. They bobbed in the water like tiny corks, but soon got the idea of swimming. Father Grebe fed one of them a small beetle he had caught. The other chicks fussed around, wanting some, too.

A shadow flickered over the pond. Mother Grebe watched, clucking her chicks close. A mother could not be too careful! It was a hawk gliding low over the marsh in search of mice or voles. Then she saw a mallard hustling her chicks out onto the island, quacking noisily. Something had bothered her. *Cluck-quick,* Mother Grebe seemed to say. Her chicks scrambled up on her back, and she ferried them quickly home to the nest. It was the safest place to be when a snapping turtle was on the prowl.

About Grebes

Nest
A pair of grebes builds a well-hidden floating nest—like a small private island—out of rushes and sedges. They anchor the nest to standing reeds.

Eggs
A female pied-billed grebe usually lays from four to seven bluish eggs. Parents share sitting duty. The female takes longer turns. When she leaves, she covers the eggs to hide them.

My Space!
Grebes guard an area around their nest site. It is their territory.

Neighbors
Many ducks feed in the open water along with the grebes. Dabbling ducks, such as mallards, pintails, and teal, upend to feed. Then all you see are tails! They eat water plants and seeds, snails, leeches, worms, and insects.

Splatter, Splash!

A grebe's legs are set far back on its body and its toes have lobes. This makes it a strong diver and swimmer. When it comes to flying, it is hard for the grebe to take off. It splashes for a long way across the water.

Food

Grebes eat small fish, crayfish, dragonfly and damselfly larvae, water boatmen, snails, diving beetles, frogs, and some water plants.

What a Voice!

Grebes are silent except at nesting time, when they call: *cuck, cuck, cuck, cow, cow, cow, cow-ah, cow-ah.* They sound spooky.

Dabchick

The pied-billed grebe (in the story) is named for its two-colored beak, or bill. The bird is called water witch and dabchick, too.

Going Down

Grebes dive well, even with young aboard! If a hawk threatens from above, a grebe flattens its feathers, squeezing out air that helps it float. It slowly sinks in the water.

Turtle's Travels

Food was so-o easy to find in midsummer!
The pond seethed with insects, tadpoles, snails,
and little fish. In no time at all, Turtle had eaten
enough. Claws scrabbling, she scuffled onto a
slimy floating log and settled down to bask.
Only twice did she plop off her log—once
when a shadow-of-hawk passed, and again when
a short, sharp rain fell. She needed an all-day
siesta to rest up for her coming journey.

Late afternoon, Turtle headed for the shore. She swam past the water lilies, through a floating jungle of bladderwort and bur reed, into the shallows. What a tangle! She pushed by a clump of pickerelweed and plodded up the steep slope. On and on she trudged, not stopping until she reached a sandy bank on the edge of the fields. The soil was damp—good for digging.

Turtle dug with her hind claws, flicking soil back without looking. When her nest was smooth and about three inches deep, she laid six leathery eggs in it. With great care, she covered the eggs with soil and stomped it flat. She scuffled dead leaves and grasses over the diggings to disguise them. Her job of mothering was done.

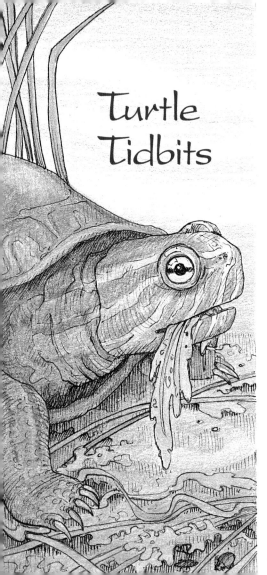

Turtle Tidbits

On the Menu

Insects, tadpoles, snails, fish, cattail seeds and stems, algae (green slime), and even dead animals are part of a turtle's varied diet.

No Teeth

Turtles tear their food with horny "beaks."

Mobile Home

A turtle can't come out of its shell, which is part of the turtle's skeleton. The top shell has an outside layer of horny scales and an inside layer of bone, which is fused to flattened ribs.

Short Stack?

Turtles can't make their own body heat. They bask in the sun to warm their bodies and strengthen their shells. Safe basking places—on logs, rocks, and muskrat or beaver lodges—may be in short supply. So the turtles clamber on top of one another.

Long Rest

Turtles hibernate in mud at the bottom of the pond. It is warmer than the water! They cannot breathe with their lungs underwater. They get enough oxygen from the water through the skin of their mouths and throats.

Ice Magic

Ice is lighter than water and floats. If this were not so, ponds would freeze from the bottom up. Fish, frogs, turtles, and pond insects could not survive.

Predators

Skunks, foxes, raccoons, badgers, and ground squirrels dig up and eat turtle eggs. Wading birds, frogs, fish, and snakes eat hatchlings and young turtles.

Marathon!

A newly hatched turtle's first task is to find water. It can be a long and dangerous journey. Scientists do not know for sure how turtles find the way. They might head for moonlight reflected in the pond.

Waterweed Jungle

Diving Beetle lived among a tangle of weeds not far from the shore. Sometimes a water strider skittered by on its long legs, making shadowy dimples. Other times whirligigs near the lily pads swam tight circles in search of food. Mostly, this was a calm, quiet-seeming place. But down below, it was a jungle! And Diving Beetle was one of the fiercest hunters in it!

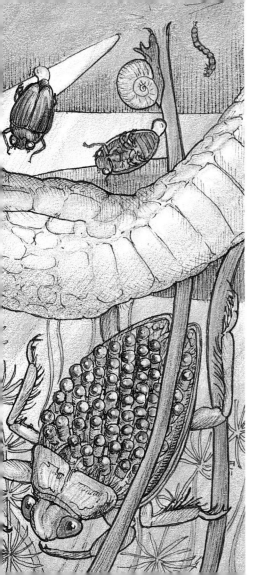

Many other kinds of beetles and bugs lived among the weeds. Tadpoles that looked like wiggly commas grazed the water plants for slime. Shoals of minnows darted through the weed forest, catching the light as they turned. Caddis fly larvae crawled along in their twiggy cases. Diving Beetle had his choice of prey. He scuttled through the weeds, using his back legs like tiny oars, and snatched a small tadpole to eat.

A hunting snake passed overhead, disturbing a mass of mosquito wigglers dangling from the surface by their tails—breathing. The wigglers sank down into the weeds. A giant water bug sped by, his back covered with his mate's eggs. Diving Beetle went on hunting. He had plenty of air trapped under his wing cases to stay down in his jungle for hours.

Jungle Monsters

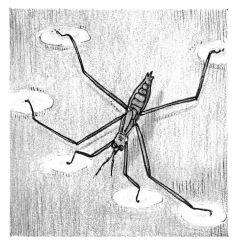

Life Cycle

A diving beetle begins its life as an egg laid in a plant stem or in water. It hatches into a larva called a water tiger. The larva eats and eats and sheds its skin to grow. It crawls from the pond, burrows into moist soil, becomes a pupa, and at last hatches into a beetle.

Skate Champions!

How can water striders skitter across the water without sinking? Their bristly feet spread their weight and trap small cushions of air that keep them from piercing the surface "skin" of the water.

Whirligigs

Whirligig beetles glean hatching midges and other small insects from the water surface. Their spinning may help them "round up" prey. They have split eyes that see under and above water at the same time.

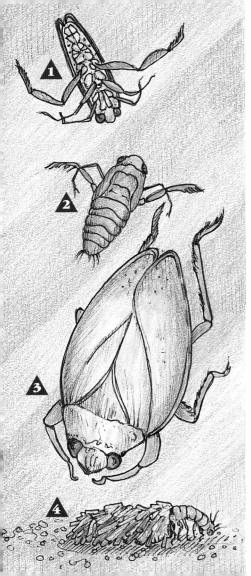

More Insects

1 Backswimmers swim upside down with jerky strokes using their bristle-fringed hind legs as oars.

2 Water boatmen swim right side up and paddle with middle and hind legs.

3 Giant water bugs are also called "toe biters." They eat tadpoles, fish, and insects. Some males carry their mate's eggs cemented to their backs to keep them safe.

4 Caddis fly larvae glue tiny pebbles or twigs into cone-shaped, spiral "jackets" to protect their soft bodies.

Snorkel Tail

A water scorpion looks a bit like a stick insect. It has a long, tail-like breathing tube. It pokes this "snorkel" through the surface film to breathe.

Snails

Snails are part of the pond's cleanup crew. They scrape algae off leaves, stems, logs, and rocks, and eat it.

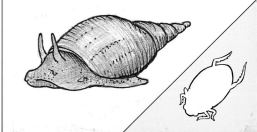

Gone Fishing

Heron stretched his neck and ruffled his wings.
He tweaked a feather into place with his beak.
Dawn was painting the sky with pale golden
streaks. It was time to go fishing! He flapped
from his treetop perch. With slow, graceful wing
beats, he soon arrived at his best fishing hole.

Kok, kok, kok. A harsh voice called from the cattails. Bother! A bittern was here first. Heron touched down on his lanky legs a little farther along the shore, startling a snipe that flew off with a harsh *skipe* call. Heron settled his wings and waded slowly, so-o slowly in the shallows, scarcely rippling the mirror-water. He stopped, statue-still, and watched for shimmery fish-flashes.

Jab! He thrust his beak deep into the weeds to snap up an unwary crayfish. Stab! He speared a bluegill. Bluegills were such finny fish! Heron dropped his catch for an instant. He snatched it up again, headfirst, so fish fins would not catch in his throat. Gulp! A bulge traveled down Heron's snaky neck as he swallowed. Yum! Good breakfast.

About Herons

Nests

Herons usually build straggly nests in treetop colonies with other herons. They find sticks on the ground or steal them from neighbors!

Family Life

Male and female herons both care for eggs and chicks. Their three to four blue-green eggs hatch in about a month. Chicks are ungainly, scrawny, and always hungry. The parents throw up partly digested fish into the chicks' mouths. Later they dump whole fish into the nest and let the chicks fight over them.

Beaks and Feet

A heron's beak is strong and sharp, great for stabbing slippery fish. Long-toed feet spread the heron's weight so it does not sink much into mud. Long legs allow the heron to wade in belly-deep water!

Enemies

Crows and ravens eat herons' eggs. Eagles, red-tailed hawks, vultures, raccoons, and bears prey on nestlings. If a heron survives its first year, it can live more than twenty years.

Food Fight?

Herons, kingfishers, grebes, and other birds all eat fish. You might think there would not be enough food for all of them.

Most of the time the birds avoid fighting over food by using different parts of the pond, catching prey in different ways, and hunting at different times of day.

Something Fishy

Herons eat fish, frogs, toads, small turtles, voles, mice, baby birds, and insects.

Fair Shares

Each kind of fish-eating bird has its own special fishing style. A heron stalks and jabs or "freezes" and stabs. A grebe dives from a swimming position. A kingfisher dives from its perch and catches small fish with its beak. It eats back at the perch.

Muskrat's Morning

Muskrat lived in a stretch of the marsh between a cattail bed and a small island. This morning she planned to scent-mark some boundary places with musk to remind muskrat neighbors to keep out. But first, food! She gnawed a chunk of cattail stem and towed it to her nearest feeding platform. Scrabbling out of the water, she held the stem in her paws. She stripped away the tough outer leaves, nibbling only the juicy bits inside.

Tsuk, tsuk. A wren buzzed in alarm. Muskrat quit munching mid-mouthful. Was Fox prowling? Was Raccoon about? Home was not as safe as before.

After a hot summer, the pond had shrunk. The mud flats where the sandpipers foraged had dried and split into curly crusts. Muskrat could no longer reach her bank den from the water. The channel she had dug was high and dry. Too bad! It had been a cozy home for her and the babies, with its three chambers. Now she had to build a new house in deeper water for safety.

All morning Muskrat clipped and snipped, towed and tugged, piling cattails onto a mud mound. The pile grew. Soon she had the start of a fine lodge. She hollowed out a room inside, above waterline, and dug doors underwater for safe homecomings. Yes, this would be a good winter home!

More About Muskrats

Families

A mother muskrat gives birth to 4 to 7—sometimes up to 11—babies in a litter. Babies are born almost naked, helpless, and blind. After 2 weeks their eyes open. They can dive and swim. A female muskrat may have up to 5 litters a year. Wow!

Neighbors

Many birds (especially ducks), snakes, snapping turtles, frogs, toads, and skunks may bask or snooze on muskrat houses or live inside them—even when the muskrats are there!

Teeth

A muskrat's lips close behind its sharp, ratlike front teeth so it can gnaw plants underwater and not swallow water as well.

Hungry, Hungry!

Left alone, some ponds fill with mud made from dead plants. Live plants start to grow far out in the water. In time, the pond becomes a marsh, then a meadow. Munching muskrats help keep the pond open. If *too many* muskrats are born, they eat so much that food runs out! The muskrats must move—even cross-country—to a new home.

Enemies

Mink, hawks and owls, coyotes, foxes, weasels, dogs, raccoons, snakes, and snapping turtles prey on muskrats.

Tales of Tails

Muskrats have scaly tails that are flattened side to side. They use their tails as rudders to steer when turning.

A beaver's tail is like a flat paddle. It helps the beaver balance on land when it is chomping trees. The tail is a fat store. Beavers warn other beavers of danger with a loud tail slap on the water. *Splash!* The sound carries far.

Marsh Munchies

Muskrats are mainly plant eaters. They eat juicy roots, shoots, and stems of water plants. When plants are scarce they may eat fish, frogs, clams, crayfish, young birds, and carrion (dead animals). Beavers feast on tender aspen and willow bark.

Animals All Around

Each muddy bank, fallen snag, cattail marsh, and quiet bay shelters countless creatures. Anywhere you go, there are more animals around than you see. Here are others you might meet around a pond.

Moose

These huge, gangly animals live in spacious areas in northern North America and the Rocky Mountains. They feed in woodlands and marshy ponds and lakes.

Moose are tall—more than six feet tall to their shoulders, not counting their heads and antlers! They could not fit through your front door.

Milkweed Beetles

These beetles feed on poisonous milkweed plants that make them taste bad to birds. Their bright patterns warn birds to leave them be.

Mosquitoes

We think of them as pests, but mosquito eggs, larvae, and adults are important links in the pond food chain.

Snapping Turtles

"Snappers" like to rest in the mud, with only eyes and nostrils showing. They have huge heads and jaws. Besides eating plants, they eat insects, fish, young muskrats, and birds—often snapping up ducklings from below.

Crayfish

These lobster look-alikes live in holes in muddy pond banks or under rocks. A tail-flick propels them backward to escape danger.

River Otters

These sleek, playful mammals live in ponds and rivers where they have wildness and space.

Did You Find?

Bear

Deer

Fox

Mink

Canada goose

Bittern

Hawk

Killdeer

Wren

Water snake

Chorus frog

Fish

Insects galore! (Ladybug, cricket, damselfly, mayfly, beetle, grasshopper, mosquitoes)

Baby Boom

A pond habitat suits many animals, with its meadows, marsh, and open water, and all the busy edges in between. It is a great place to raise a family. Not all the young grow up in the same way.

▲ Some young hatch from fragile or leathery eggs. Whether they have feathers or plated shells, you can tell from the start what they will grow up to be.

▲ Some young are born live. They are furry, are fed milk, and look like small versions of their parents.

△ Other young look nothing like their parents. As larvae they live and act differently than adults.

Can you match △-adults with the correct △-young?

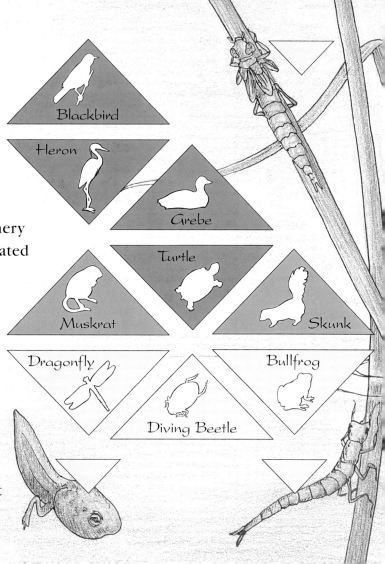

Blackbird

Heron

Grebe

Turtle

Muskrat

Skunk

Dragonfly

Bullfrog

Diving Beetle